Mathamazing

Raymond Blum

Illustrated by Jeff Sinclair

Sterling Publishing Co., Inc.
New York

10 9 8 7 6 5 4 3 2 1

Published 2002 by Sterling Publishing Company, Inc.
387 Park Avenue South, New York, NY 10016
Originally published under the title *Math Tricks, Puzzles & Games*
©1994 by Raymond Blum
Illustrations © 1994 by Jeff Sinclair
Distributed in Canada by Sterling Publishing
℅ Canadian Manda Group, One Atlantic Avenue, Suite 105
Toronto, Ontario, Canada M6K 3E7
Distributed in Great Britain and Europe by Chris Lloyd
at Orca Book Services, Stanley House, Fleets Lane, Poole BH15 3AJ,
England
Distributed in Australia by Capricorn Link (Australia) Pty. Ltd.
P.O. Box 704, Windsor, NSW 2756 Australia

Sterling ISBN 1-4027-0026-1

DEDICATION

This book would not have been possible without the incredible support and encouragement from my wife, Gerri, and my daughter, Katie. With loving gratitude, I dedicate this book to them.

INTRODUCTION—A NOTE TO PARENTS AND TEACHERS

All of the math activities in this book have one thing in common, *they are fun!* This book is filled with mysterious magic tricks, exciting games, fascinating puzzles, and humorous riddles. Children of all abilities, ages nine and up, will enjoy this entertaining collection of number fun.

The activities have clear, uncomplicated, step-by-step instructions so that they are easy for children to read and understand. There is a glossary for looking up unfamiliar words. Any needed supplies can easily be found in the home or purchased at minimal cost. The book is organized so that children can open it up, pick out an activity, and get started on their own. They will enjoy sharing these fascinating activities with their family and friends or their entire class.

I discovered early in my teaching career that children will learn if they are properly motivated. When learning is fun and exciting, they become interested and want to learn. This book helps provide that motivation. All of the activities have been classroom tested and math teachers at any level can use this book to create interest and stimulate learning.

CONTENTS

1.
CARD TRICKS

Card tricks are the most popular of all magic tricks. They can be performed anywhere and a regular deck of cards is all that is needed.

These card tricks are easy to learn and perform. No sleight of hand is required and, if you carefully follow the steps, they practically work themselves.

The tricks are organized from the easiest to the hardest, so choose those that are right for you. Even though the tricks are easy to learn, be sure to practice them by yourself first. When you have worked a trick through successfully two or three times, you are ready to perform it for others.

Never repeat a card trick for the same person or they might figure out the trick's secret. Perform a second trick instead, and everyone will have twice as much fun!

7–11

You will amaze your friends with your psychic powers when you look into the future and correctly predict the outcome of this card trick!

Materials

A deck of playing cards
An envelope

Paper and pencil

Preparation

Remove 9 red cards and 9 black cards from the deck.

Write "THERE WILL BE 2 MORE BLACK CARDS IN THE LONG ROW THAN RED CARDS IN THE SHORT ROW!" on a piece of paper and then seal it inside an envelope.

Presentation

1. Tell your friend that you have predicted the outcome of this trick and that you have sealed the prediction inside an envelope.

2. Hand him the 18 cards and ask him to shuffle them thoroughly.

3. Tell him to deal the cards face up in 2 rows in any order that he chooses. The first row should have 7 cards and the second row should have 11 cards.

4. Finally, remind your friend that he was free to choose the cards that were dealt into each row. Then open up your prediction and show him that it is correct. Your friend will think that you possess supernatural powers!

The Secret

The difference in the lengths of the rows determines the prediction. $11 - 7 = 4$ and half of 4 is 2. So there will always be 2 more blacks in the long row than reds in the short row. Also, there will be 2 more reds in the long row than blacks in the short row.

A Variation

Start with 15 red cards and 15 black cards. Put 11 cards in the short row and 19 cards in the long row and see how your prediction changes.

There will be four more black cards in the long row than red cards in the short row.

RIDDLE ME

Why is it dangerous to do math in the jungle?

If you multiply 4 and 2 you will get 8 (ate)!

9

TREE OF CLUBS

You secretly predict which card will be chosen from the deck. It looks as if the "Number Spirits" have played a trick on you when your friend's chosen card doesn't match your prediction—or does it?

Materials

An envelope   A glue stick
A deck of playing cards with a Joker

Preparation

Photocopy the card on this page, cut around it and then glue or laminate it over the Joker. Seal this card inside an envelope.

Put the 3 of Clubs on top of the deck and put the 8 of Clubs in the ninth position down from the top of the deck.

Presentation

1. Tell your friend that he will randomly select a card from the deck and that the card in the envelope will match his selected card.

2. Ask him for a number *between* 10 and 20. (*Caution:* Between does not include 10 or 20.)

Example

17

3. Deal that many cards into a small pile, one card at a time.

4. Ask your friend to find the sum of the digits of his number.

$$17 \rightarrow 1 + 7 = 8$$

5. Return that many cards to the top of the big pile, one card at a time.

Return 8 cards

6. Put the rest of the small pile on top of the big pile.

7. Pretend to perform some supernatural hocus-pocus as you ask the "Number Spirits" for a sign that will tell your friend how many cards he should count down in the deck. Pretend that they tell you to turn over the top card. It will be the 8 of Clubs. This sign means that your friend should count down 8 cards in the deck and turn over the eighth card. It will be the 3 of Clubs.

8. Finally, remind your friend that he was free to choose any number. Then open up the envelope and pull out the Tree of Clubs. Act surprised and upset, and then blame the "Number Spirits" for switching cards and playing a mean trick on you. But wait! The trick worked after all!

The 3 of Clubs = The Tree of Clubs

The Secret
This trick uses a mathematical procedure called casting out nines. Any number between 10 and 20 minus the sum of its digits always equals 9.

MIND READER

This is a trick that you and your friend can perform together. After you leave the room, your friend asks someone to choose a card from the 9 cards that are on the table. When you return, not a single word is spoken, yet you are able to reveal the chosen card!

Materials
A deck of playing cards

Preparation
Practice with your friend before performing the trick for others.

Presentation
1. Remove any 9 cards from the deck. Then place them face up on the table in a 3 by 3 array as shown here. Give the rest of the deck to your friend to hold.

2. After you leave the room, your friend asks someone to point to one of the 9 cards.

3. When you return, pretend that you are reading your friend's mind and then reveal the chosen card.

The Secret

Imagine that the top of the deck that your friend is holding is divided into 9 equal sections. These 9 sections correspond to the 3 by 3 array of cards on the table. Your friend signals you by simply holding her thumb over one of the imaginary sections. This tells you which card was chosen.

Example

Chosen card

Your friend's signal

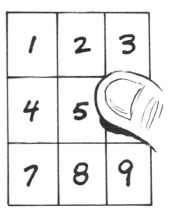

Your friend holds her thumb over the imaginary section 6 on the top of the deck. She should hold the deck so that you can easily read the signal, but at the same time, not be too obvious and give away the secret. With a little practice, you will be able to read anyone's mind!

LAST CARD

Your friend will be mystified when you correctly predict the number of cards that she secretly removes from the deck!

Materials
A deck of playing cards with a Joker
A glue stick

Preparation
Photocopy the card on this page, cut the card out and then glue or laminate it over one of the Jokers.

Put this card in the twenty-first position down from the top of the deck.

Presentation
1. Hand your friend the deck of cards. When your back is turned, ask her to remove from 1 to 15 cards from the *top* of the deck. Tell her to hide them in her hand.

2. Turn around and ask her to concentrate on the number of cards that she removed. Pretend that you are reading her mind as you *quietly* deal out 20 cards, one at

14

a time, face down on the table. Put this pack of 20 cards in your hand and then set the rest of the deck aside.

3. Tell your friend to turn her cards over one at a time on the table. Every time she turns over a card, turn over the top card from your pack and put it face up on top of hers.

4. Continue turning over cards until hers are all gone. When she runs out of cards your next card will say, "THAT WAS YOUR LAST CARD!" It works every time, no matter how many cards your friend removes!

The Secret

When you count out 20 cards, their order is reversed. This puts the "THAT WAS YOUR LAST CARD!" card a certain number down from the top. That number will always equal the number of cards that your friend removes.

FAVORITE NUMBER

Pick any number from 1 to 9. See what happens when you multiply that number by 259 and by 429. After you get the answer, clear your calculator. Then multiply 259 × 429 and you will see why it works.

YOUR SELECTED CARD IS . . .

Your friend secretly chooses a card from a deck of cards. When a magical phrase is spelled out, your friend's chosen card suddenly appears!

Materials

A complete deck of 52 playing cards with no Jokers

Presentation

1. Hand your friend a deck of cards, and tell her to shuffle them thoroughly.

2. Ask her to try to cut the deck into two equal packs. (It does not matter if the packs are equal, but each one should have between 20 and 30 cards.)

Example: 28 cards and 24 cards

3. Tell her to choose either pack and put the other pack aside until later.

4. Ask her to count the cards in her pack to see how close she got to 26. (If her pack does not have between 20 and 30 cards, ask her to start over and cut the entire deck again.)

16

5. Suppose your friend chooses the pack of 28 cards. Ask her to find the sum of the digits of that number.

28 → 2 + 8 = 10

6. Tell her to deal that many cards into a small pile, and then memorize the top card of that pile. Have her put the rest of her pack on top of this small pile.

7. Ask her to put her pack on top of the other pack that she did not choose, and then hand you the entire deck of cards.

8. Explain to your friend that you are going to spell out a magical phrase that will help you find her card. Deal cards from the top of the deck, one at a time, as you spell this phrase out loud: "Y-O-U-R S-E-L-E-C-T-E-D C-A-R-D I-S." Turn over 1 card for each letter of the phrase. The *next card* is your friend's selected card!

The Secret

This trick uses a mathematical procedure called casting out nines. Any number between 20 and 30 minus the sum of its digits always equals 18. This equals the number of letters in the magical phrase.

RIDDLE ME

What did the acorn say when it grew up?

Gee, I'm a tree (geometry)!

COME FORTH

Your friend will be astonished when you command his chosen card to come forth, and it rises up out of the deck!

Materials

A complete deck of 52 playing cards with no Jokers

Presentation

1. Have your friend shuffle the cards as many times as he wants. When he is finished, tell him to memorize the *bottom card*. **Example: Ace of Hearts**

2. Ask him to put the deck on the table and turn over the top 3 cards.

3. Tell your friend to deal cards face down below each of these 3 cards. He should start with the number on the face-up card (Aces = 1, Jacks = 11, Queens = 12, and Kings = 13), and then keep dealing cards until he gets to 15. For example, if the face-up card is a 9, he would deal 6 more cards to get to 15.

Example

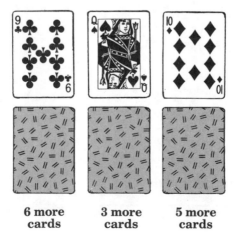

4. Ask him to keep the 3 face-up cards on the table, and then put all the face-down cards on the *bottom* of the deck.

(12)

5. Have him find the sum of the 3 face-up cards. (**9 + Q + 10 = 31**) Tell him to deal out that many cards, and then put them on the *bottom* of the deck.

6. Explain that you have supernatural powers and that you can force any card to come out of the deck on your command. Ask your friend for the name of his card so that you can command it to come out. He says, "It was the Ace of Hearts."

7. Pretend to do some hocus-pocus as you say, "Ace of Hearts, come forth!" Repeat your command, and then look pleased with the result.

8. Your friend, of course, won't see anything happen, but you insist that his card did come forth. Turn over cards off the top of the deck one at a time and say, "Here's the first card, here's the second, here's the third, and the Ace of Hearts comes FOURTH!" Turn over the fourth card and it will be your friend's card!

The Secret
Each face-up card + counting up to 15 + the value of the card = 16. So 16 × 3 face-up cards = 48. Then 48 + 4 (come fourth) = 52 cards in the deck.

19

WIZARD OF ODDS

You and your friend each select a card from your own deck of cards. The probability that you will select identical cards is 1 out of 2,704. But for some magical reason, you are able to beat the odds every time!

Materials

2 decks of playing cards without Jokers

Presentation

1. Have two decks of cards on the table, one for you and one for your friend.

2. Tell your friend to do exactly what you do. If you shuffle your deck, she should shuffle her deck. If you turn your deck around, she should turn her deck around, and so on.

3. This part of the trick is nothing more than a little hocus-pocus. Shuffle, double cut, turn, shuffle again, and triple cut your deck. Make sure that your friend does the same with her deck.

4. Flip your deck over, and then turn your deck clockwise and then counterclockwise 2 or 3 times. She should be doing the same with her deck. While you are doing this, it is very important that you *memorize your friend's bottom card*—this is your *key card*.

5. Turn your deck face down once again. Then pick out a card from near the center of your deck. Pretend that you are memorizing your card (but you only need to remember the key card on the bottom of your friend's deck) and then place it *on top of your deck*. Your friend does the same with her deck.

6. Each of you should cut your deck in half once so that the chosen cards are lost in the middle of their decks. This puts the key card on top of her chosen card.

7. Finally, exchange decks with your friend. Tell your friend to find her card and that you will find yours. Look through the cards until you see the key card. Your friend's chosen card will be the card *to the right* of the key card. Pretend that her chosen card is yours, remove it, and place it face down on the table. Your friend does the same with her card.

8. Explain to your friend that the probability of choosing identical cards is very small—1 out of 2,704 (1/52 × 1/52 = 1/2,704). Your friend won't believe her eyes when you flip the cards over and they are identical!

2.
GAMES FOR 2

Everybody loves to play games. They can be fun and exciting, especially if you have the advantage of knowing how to win every time! Most of the games in this chapter have a secret mathematical winning strategy that will allow you to win no matter what your opponent does.

Before you play a game against a friend, memorize the winning strategy and then play the game two or three times by yourself. With practice, you will be able to defeat the toughest opponent.

Don't play a game too many times with the same person or they might discover the winning secret. If your friend wants to keep playing, change to a different game. You will win that game too!

TRISKAIDEKAPHOBIA
(Fear of the Number 13)

Thirteen is one of the unluckiest numbers in the world. It will be very lucky for you, however, because you will be able to force your opponent to pick up the dreaded coin number 13 every time!

Materials
13 coins

How to Play
1. Use the coins to make a figure 13 on the table.

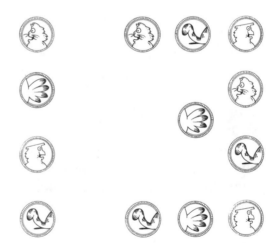

2. Flip to see who goes first. Then each player takes turns picking up coins. A player must pick up one or two coins on each turn.

3. The player who picks up the last coin on the table loses.

24

Winning Strategy

Count to yourself as coins are removed. If you pick up the key coins **3**, **6**, **9**, and **12**, you will win every time. For example, your friend goes first and picks up coins 1 and 2. On your turn, you would pick up coin 3. If your friend picks up coin 4, you would pick up coins 5 and **6**. As play continues, be sure to pick up coins **9** and **12** and your friend will be forced to pick up coin number 13!

If you go first and then your friend picks up coin 3, don't worry. You can pick up coins **6**, **9**, and **12** and still win the game. Of course, if you want to be guaranteed of winning every time, go second!

A Variation

The number 26 (two 13's) is doubly dreaded! Start with 26 coins and see if you can figure out the new winning strategy.

The key coins are: 1, 4, 7, 10, 13, 16, 19, 22, and 25.

RIDDLE ME

If 2's company and 3's a crowd, what's 4 and 5?

4 + 5 = 9!

TICK + TACK + TOE

Tick-tack-toe, or naughts and crosses, is one of the best-known games in the world. In this version, the game is played with numbers, and the first player who makes a tick-tack-toe with a sum of 15 wins the game.

Materials

Paper and pencil

How to Play

1. Draw a tick-tack-toe game board on a piece of paper. Write the even numbers and the odd numbers from 1 to 10 underneath.

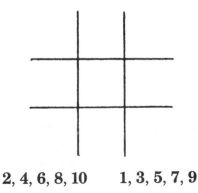

2, 4, 6, 8, 10   1, 3, 5, 7, 9

2. This game is played just like regular tick-tack-toe, but instead of using X's, one player uses the even numbers. Instead of using O's, the other player uses the odd numbers.

3. You and your friend decide who goes first. Then each player takes turns writing a number in a space. When a number is used, cross it off because it cannot be used again.

4. The winner is the first person who makes a tick-tack-toe horizontally, vertically, or diagonally, with a sum of 15. If neither player is able to make a tick-tack-toe, the game is a tie.

5. Take turns using the even numbers and the odd numbers when you play more than one game.

Winning Strategy

Try to set up winning sums in two directions. If your opponent blocks one way, you can still win with the other!

RIDDLE ME

Which insects are excellent in math?

Mosquitoes, because they add to our misery, subtract from our pleasure, divide our attention, and multiply quickly!

27

3–2–1 BLASTOFF

Players count backwards and whoever is forced to say "Zero" loses the game and is blasted into the deepest regions of outer space!

Materials

None

How to Play

1. You and your friend decide who goes first. Then each player takes turns counting backwards from 30. A player may count backwards 1, 2, or 3 numbers on each turn.

2. The player who says "Zero" is the loser.

Winning Strategy

The key numbers for this game are **29**, **25**, **21**, **17**, **13**, **9**, **5**, and of course **1**. For example, you start by saying, "30 - **29**." If your friend counts 28 - 27 - 26, you would say, "**25**." Your friend counts 24 - 23, so you would say, "22 - **21**." As you continue counting backwards, make sure that you land on the rest of the key numbers and you will win every time!

Don't worry if you don't land on all of the key numbers at first. Just pick up key numbers along the way and you will still win.

A Variation

Count backwards 1, 2, 3, *or 4* numbers on each turn and see if you can figure out the new winning strategy.

The key numbers are: 26, 21, 16, 11, 6, and 1.

ANCIENT EGYPT

This game has been played all over the world for over 3000 years. The winning player outsmarts an opponent and gets three markers in a row in any direction.

Materials

Paper and pencil   3 coins and 3 paper clips

How to Play

1. Draw an Ancient Egypt game board on a piece of paper. Make it much larger than the diagram so that six markers can freely move about it.

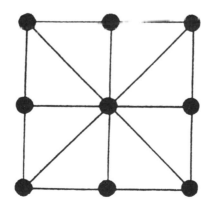

2. One player uses 3 coins for markers and the other player uses 3 paper clips.

3. Flip one of the coins to see who goes first. Then the players take turns putting their markers on the dots one at a time. (The first player is not allowed to put the first marker on the center dot.)

4. After all 6 markers are on the game board, the players take turns sliding any one of their markers along a line to the first open dot.

5. The first person to get his or her three markers in a row in any direction is the winner.

Winning Strategy
Try to set up winning situations in two directions. If your opponent blocks one of them, you can still win with the other!

A Variation
Instead of sliding markers along a line to the first open dot, you are allowed to move your marker to *any* open dot.

RIDDLE ME

There are 12 one-cent stamps in a dozen. So how many two-cent stamps are in a dozen?

12 two-cent stamps. A dozen is a dozen!

SNAKE EYES

The winner is the first person to score 100 points by rolling the dice. It is not as easy as it sounds, because there is a dangerous snake waiting to steal all of your points every time you roll the dice!

Materials

A pair of dice   Paper and pencil

How to Play

1. Make a score card with each player's name on a piece of paper.

2. Roll the dice to see who goes first. Then each player takes turns rolling the dice.

3. On your turn, roll the dice and find the sum of the top numbers. You can quit and write down that total or you can roll again. As you continue rolling the dice, keep a running total in your head. When you decide to quit, add that total to your score on the score card.

4. You can keep rolling as long as you want, but if a 1 comes up on one of the dice, you lose all your points for that turn. If two 1's come up (snake eyes), you lose all your points for the whole game and must start over again at 0!

5. The first person to score 100 or more points is the winner.

Winning Strategy

The probability of getting a 1 on one of the dice is 10 out of 36. This is about one-third. The probability of getting snake eyes is 1 out of 36. Keep this in mind as you decide how many times to roll the dice on each turn.

A Variation

Change the winning total to 250 points and count doubles as double their sum. For example, two 6's equals 12 and double that would add 24 to your total. If a 1 comes up, you still lose your points for that turn, but you don't lose all of your points when you roll two 1's. In this game, the snake is friendly and snake eyes is worth 25 points!

RIDDLE ME

Why was the math book so unhappy?

It had too many problems!

BLACK HOLE

The player who is forced down into the black hole loses the game and is never heard from again!

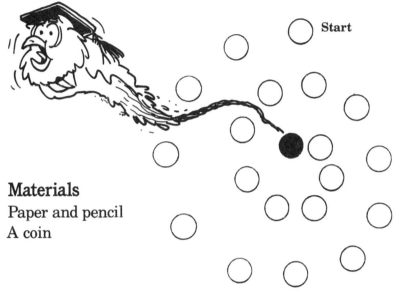

Materials
Paper and pencil
A coin

How to Play

1. Draw the Black Hole game spiral on a piece of paper. Make it much larger than the diagram so that a coin can freely move from one circle to the next.

2. Flip the coin to see who goes first. Then each player takes turns moving the coin from circle to circle. A player may move the coin one or two circles on each turn.

3. The player who lands in the black hole loses the game.

Winning Strategy

The key numbers for this game are **1**, **4**, **7**, **10**, **13**, **16**, and **19**. Count to yourself as the coin moves around the spiral and try to land on as many key numbers as possible. For example, your friend goes first and moves to circle 2. On your turn, you would move two places to circle **4**. Then, if your friend moves to circle 6, you would move one place to circle **7**. As play continues, make sure that you land on the rest of the key numbers, and your opponent will be forced into the black hole every time!

A Variation

Make it a counting game and whoever says 20 is the *winner*. See if you can figure out the new key numbers, and then call your friend on the phone and try it out.

The key numbers are: 2, 5, 8, 11, 14, 17, and 20.

LAS VEGAS

Dice are rolled and cards are turned over just like in a Las Vegas gambling casino. Your odds of winning, however, are much better in this game.

Materials

A deck of playing cards   2 dice

How to Play

1. From the deck, select 22 cards—the 2, 3, 4, 5, 6, 7, 8, 9, 10, Jack (11) and Queen (12) of Clubs and Hearts. Set the rest of the deck aside.

2. Each player picks a suit, and both lay their 11 cards face up in order in front of them.

3. Roll the dice to see who goes first. Then each player takes turns rolling the dice. On a turn, a player rolls the dice and finds the sum of the top numbers. Then he turns over his card that equals that sum. For example, if he rolls a 4 and a 3, he would turn over his 7 card.

4. He continues rolling the dice and turning over his cards. His turn continues until he rolls the number of a card that he has already turned over. For example, he rolls a 6 and 1. He has already turned his 7 card so it becomes his opponent's turn.

5. The game continues until one of the players turns over all of his or her cards.

Winning Strategy

There is no winning strategy for this game, but it is a good lesson in probability. There are six different ways to get a 7, so it will come up the most. There is only one way to get a 2 (snake eyes) and there is only one way to get a 12 (boxcars), so they will come up the least.

A Variation

When all the remaining numbers are less than seven, play with only one die.

ALPHABET RACE

It's a race to the end of the alphabet and the player who zaps the letter Z is the winner.

Materials
Paper and pencil

How to Play
1. Write the entire alphabet on a piece of paper.

2. You and your friend decide who goes first. Then each player takes turns crossing off letters of the alphabet *in order* from A to Z. A player may cross off 1, 2, 3, or 4 letters on each turn.

3. The player who crosses off the letter Z is the winner.

Winning Strategy
If you cross off the key letters **A**, **F**, **K**, **P**, **U**, and of course **Z**, you will win every time. For example, you go first and cross off **A**. If your friend crosses off B, C, and

D, you would cross off E and **F**. Your friend crosses off G, so you would cross off H, I, J, and **K**. As you continue crossing off letters, make sure that you cross off **P** and **U**, and you will be the one who crosses off the **Z**!

If your friend goes first and crosses off the **A**, you can still win. Just make sure that you pick up other key letters along the way.

Here's an easy way to remember the key letters. It's called a mnemonic aid. Just memorize this silly phrase and you will remember the key letters. They are the first letters of each word.

A Fat Kangaroo Picks Up Zebras!

GO-MOKU

Go-Moku is a board game from the Far East that has been played for thousands of years. The first player to get five marks in a row either vertically, horizontally, or diagonally wins the game.

Materials

Graph paper   2 pencils

How to Play

1. Fold a piece of graph paper in half one way and then the other, and you will have four Go-Moku game boards.

2. This game is played just like regular tick-tack-toe except that there are hundreds of squares instead of just nine.

3. You and your friend decide who goes first. Then

players take turns marking their X's and O's in the squares on the graph paper.

4. The winner is the first person to make five of his or her marks in a row in any direction.

Winning Strategy

Try to set up winning situations in two directions. If your opponent blocks one way, you can still win with the other. Also, try to get four of your marks in a row with both ends open. Your opponent cannot block both ends at the same time and you will be the winner!

A Variation

If you want to play a quicker game, let *four* in a row win.

POISON TOOTHPICK

Fifteen toothpicks are lying on the table, but don't pick your teeth with any of them. One of them contains a deadly poison! That's the toothpick that your opponent will be forced to pick up!

Materials

15 toothpicks

How to Play

1. Arrange 15 toothpicks on the table as shown in the diagram.

2. You and your friend decide who goes first. Then each player takes turns removing toothpicks. You may remove as many toothpicks as you want from *any one row* on each turn.

3. The player who picks up the last toothpick loses.

Winning Strategy

Create losing patterns for your opponent. As the game progresses, leave your opponent with any of these three patterns and you will win every time!

|
| **a single file of toothpicks**
|

                         2 equal rows of toothpicks

| | | | | | | | | | | | | |
   or   or   or
| | | | | | | | | | | | | |

Any combination of 1, 2, and 3 toothpicks

Examples: | | | | | | | |

      | or | or | |

   | | | | | |

BULL'S-EYE

It's a race to see who can hit the target first by working math problems faster than their opponent.

Materials

A deck of playing cards

How to Play

1. Remove the 12 face cards from the deck and set them aside.

2. Shuffle the rest of the deck and deal four cards face down to each player. Turn the next card face up in the center of the table. This is the target number.

3. At the count of three, all players turn their cards over at the same time. Then they $+$, $-$, $\times$, or $\div$ the numbers

on their cards (Aces = 1) and try to equal the target
number. All four cards must be used!

Example

Target

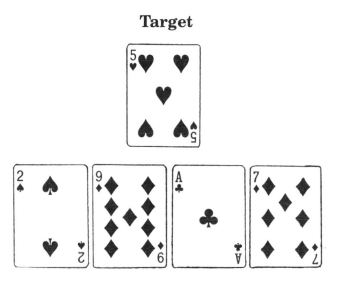

Your Hand
$$(9 - 7) \times 2 + 1 = 5$$

4. The first player to equal the target number wins a
point, and 3 points wins the game.

5. If no one can equal the target number, turn over
another card for a new target number, or redeal.

Winning Strategy

Keep rearranging your cards until you see the right
combination. Also, try to group a pair of cards together.

A Variation

If the game is too hard, put in some of the face cards.
They could be wild cards and used in your hand as any
number. If the four-card game is too easy, deal five cards
to each player.

3.
PUZZLES

If you enjoy puzzles, this chapter is for you. There are many interesting and unusual mind benders that are fun as well as challenging. They will provide hours of pleasure for problem solvers of all abilities.

You might not be able to solve some puzzles as quickly as you think, so you must be patient. If you are having trouble getting an answer, turn the page upside down, look at the hint, and try again. Some puzzles might have more than one correct solution. So your answer might be different from the one in the back of the book and still be correct.

As soon as you find some paper, a pencil, some toothpicks, and a few coins you will be ready to solve these fascinating puzzles!

LINE BOGGLERS

TWO-WAY STREET

See if you can make a third arrow that is the same size as the other two by adding only two straight lines.

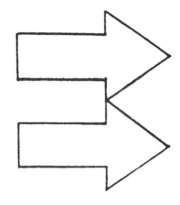

The new arrow points to the left.

SUM TIME

Add two straight lines and divide the clock face into three parts. The sum of the numbers in each part must be the same.

The sum of the numbers in each part equals 26.

6 + 5 = 9???

Can you add five straight lines to these six and get nine?

Think about the wording; get NINE.

IN NEED OF REPAIR

Add only one straight line to this equation so that it is correct.

$$1 + 3 + 5 = 148$$

Try adding the line to one of the plus signs.

TUNNELS

Try to connect each rectangle with the triangle that has the same number. Lines cannot cross or go outside the diagram.

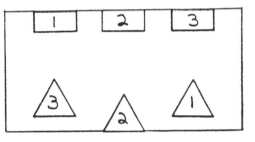

Connect the two 3's with a straight line.

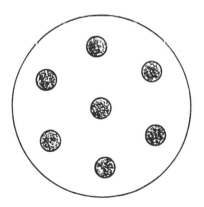

PEPPERONI PIZZA

Divide the pizza with three straight lines so that there is only one piece of pepperoni on each piece.

Start with a horizontal line just below the center piece of pepperoni.

PENCIL PUZZLES

Can you draw these figures without lifting your pencil off the paper? You are not allowed to retrace any lines but you can cross over lines.

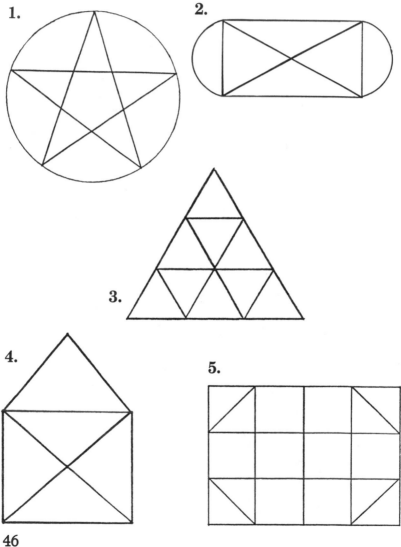

1.

2.

3.

4.

5.

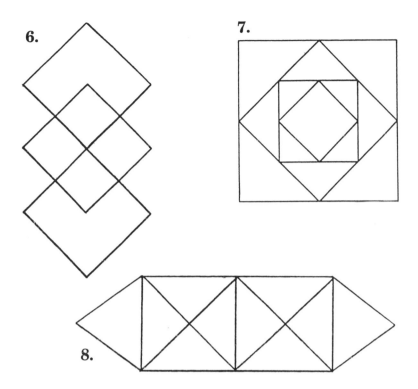

6. **7.**

8.

The Secret

Look at the points where the lines meet. They are called vertices (pronounced ver-tis-sees). Odd vertices have an odd number of lines that meet at the point.

Examples

Odd vertices

Leonard Euler (Oiler), a famous Swiss mathematician, discovered that a figure can only be traced if it has 0 or 2 odd vertices. If the figure has 0 odd vertices, start at any point and finish at that same point. If a figure has 2 odd vertices, start at one point and finish at the other.

ARCHITECT

Build a house using 11 toothpicks as shown in the diagram. See if you can make the house face the opposite direction by moving only one toothpick.

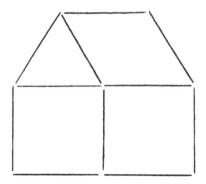

Move one of the toothpicks in the roof.

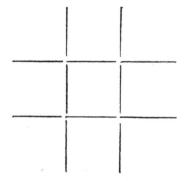

CRISSCROSS

Arrange 12 toothpicks as shown in the diagram. Can you move only three toothpicks and end up with exactly three congruent squares?

Start by moving the bottom-left toothpick.

AQUARIUM

Make a fish using eight toothpicks and a coin as shown in the diagram. Move only three toothpicks and the coin so that the fish is swimming to the right.

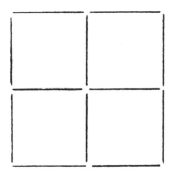

Start by moving the bottom tail toothpick.

SQUARE DEAL

The toothpicks in this diagram have been arranged to form squares. Can you remove two of the toothpicks so that only two squares remain?

Do the squares have to be congruent?

IN AND OUT

The four toothpicks in this diagram represent a wine glass with a coin inside. See if you can move two toothpicks so that the coin is *outside* the glass.

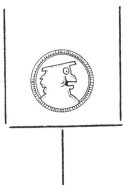

The glass will be upside down.

EQUILATERAL TRIANGLES

Arrange 16 toothpicks as shown in the diagram. Remove four toothpicks so that only four triangles remain.

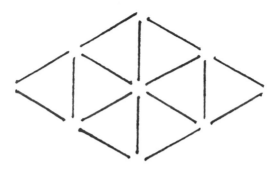

Do all the triangles have to be congruent?

COIN BAFFLERS

OVER EASY

Can you make the left triangle look like the right triangle by moving only three coins?

Start by moving the top coin.

FOUR ACROSS

Arrange six coins in the shape of a cross. There are four coins in one direction and three coins in the other. Try to move only one coin so that there are four coins in each direction.

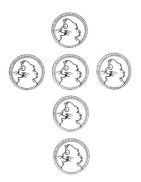

Move the bottom coin.

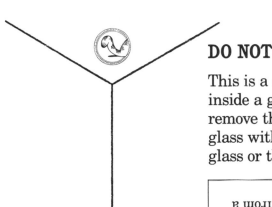

DO NOT TOUCH

This is a drawing of a coin inside a glass. Can you remove the coin from the glass without touching the glass or the coin?

Look at the glass from a different angle.

CONSTELLATION

Draw a constellation puzzle on a piece of paper. Make it much larger than the diagram so that four coins can freely move from one circle to the next. Put two like coins on circles 2 and

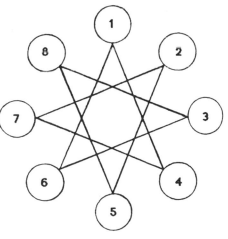

51

8, and put two other like coins on circles 4 and 6.

The object is to make the two top coins change places with the two bottom coins by sliding them, one at a time, along the lines from circle to circle. You can slide a coin as many times as you like, but coins can only be moved to open circles.

Start by moving 2 to 7. Then move 8 to 5 to 2.

COIN CHECKERS

Draw a coin checkers puzzle on a piece of paper. Make it large enough so that four coins can freely move from space to space. Place the four coins on the puzzle as shown in the diagram, heads on the left and tails on the right.

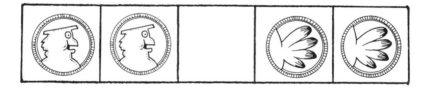

See if you can make the heads and tails change places. The moves for this puzzle are like the moves in checkers. You can slide any coin to an open space next to it, or you can jump any coin over the coin next to it into an open space. The record for this puzzle is *8 moves*. If it takes you more than 8 moves, keep trying and see if you can get it.

Start by moving a heads into the empty space and then jump it with a tails.

52

NUMBER JUGGLING

BOX SCORE

Use each of the numbers from 1 through 8. See if you can put a different number in each box so that no two consecutive numbers are touching—*not even at their corners.* For example, the box with the 5 cannot touch the box with the 4 or the 6.

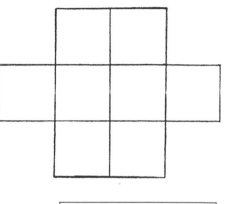

Put the 1 in one of the two center boxes.

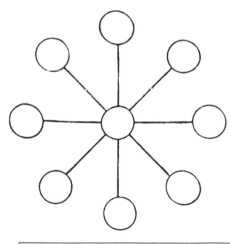

WHEEL NUMBERS

Use each of the numbers from 1 through 9. Put a different number in each circle so that the sum of each straight row of three circles is 15.

Find the center number first.

BERMUDA TRIANGLE

Use each of the numbers from 1 through 9. Can you put a different number in each circle so that the sum of each side of the triangle is 17?

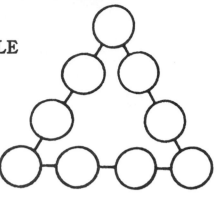

Put the 1 in one of the corners.

TROUBLESUM

Use each of the numbers from 1 through 9. See if you can put a different number in each box so that the total is 900.

$$+ \boxed{}\,\boxed{}\,\boxed{}$$

9 0 0

You will carry 2 each time.

RIDDLE ME

How many feet are in a yard?

It depends on how many kids are playing in the yard at the time!

MAGIC SQUARE

Use each of the numbers from 1 through 9. Can you put a different number in each box so that the sum of each row, column, and diagonal is 15?

Find the center number first.

HEXAGRAM

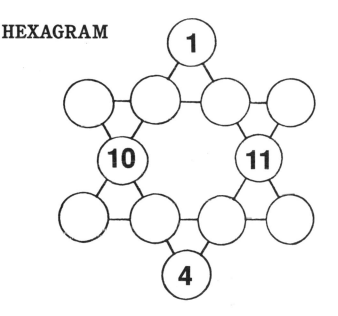

Use each of the numbers from 1 through 12. Put a different number in each circle so that the sum of each straight row of four circles is 26. Four numbers have been filled in to get you started.

BRAIN BUSTERS

STARGAZER

See if you can draw this
figure without lifting your
pencil off the paper. You
are not allowed to retrace
any lines but you can cross
over lines.

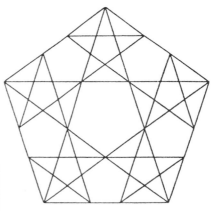

There are no odd vertices,
so start at any point and
finish at that same point.

BOX SCORE II

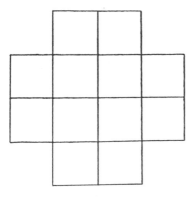

Use each of the numbers
from 1 through 12. Put
a different number in
each box so that no two
consecutive numbers are
touching—*not even at their
corners*. For example, the
box with the 11 cannot
touch the box with the 10
or the 12.

Put the 1 in one of the four center boxes.

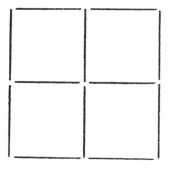

WINDOWPANES

Arrange 12 toothpicks as shown in the diagram. Can you move only four toothpicks and end up with exactly ten squares? No, you cannot break any toothpicks in half!

Do all the squares have to be congruent?

DOT TO DOT

Try to connect all nine dots using only four straight lines. Lines can cross, but you cannot lift your pencil off the paper or retrace any lines.

Try not to picture a square in your mind. See only dots and empty space.

RIDDLE ME

Why is the U.S. nickel coin smarter than the penny?

Because the nickel has more cents (sense)!

TUNNELS II

See if you can connect each square with the triangle that has the same number. Lines cannot cross or go outside the diagram.

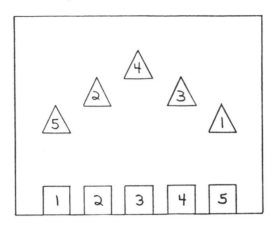

Connect the two 2's with a straight line.

TETRAHEDRON

Can you think of a way to make *four* triangles, all the *same size* as those shown, with only six toothpicks?

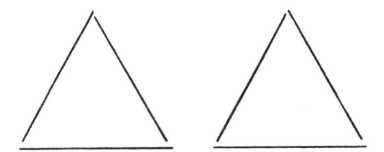

Look up the definition of tetrahedron in the glossary.

4.
FUNNY BUSINESS

Here are some silly pranks that you can use to fool your family, friends, and math teacher. These amusing tricks can be performed by themselves or used as follow-up jokes when someone asks you to repeat a card trick, an arithmetrick, or a calculator trick. Either way, they will be a lot of fun for everyone!

Try this one for starters.

MULTIPLICATION MADNESS

Did you know that $6 \times 5 = 8 \times 4$? Your friends won't believe it either, but you can prove it for them. Here's how.

$$6 \times 5 = 30 \text{ and } 8 \times 4 = 32 \text{ (it's 30 too!)}$$

I'VE GOT 11 FINGERS!?!

Your friends will think that they have lost their minds when you prove to them that you have eleven fingers!

Hold up both of your hands in front of your friend and ask, "How many fingers do you see?" She, of course, will say, "10."

You reply, "10? Let's see." Count backwards from 10, one finger at a time, on your right hand. Then add the five fingers on your left hand and you will get a total of 11 fingers!

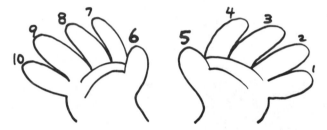

"10, 9, 8, 7, **6**, plus **5** on my left hand equals **11!?!**"

SIMPLE MATH

$$1 + 9 + 1 + 9 + 1$$

Give your friend exactly 30 seconds to figure out what simple operation can be performed on these numbers so that they will equal 15. Tell him that he cannot cross off or add any new numbers. It's easy. Just turn the page upside down!

FAST TALKER

Your friends will be amazed when you count up to 500 in only five seconds! Tell them that you will start at one and count by ones, one number at a time. Count very quickly up to twenty as an example. Explain that in exactly five seconds, you will count up to a number between four and five hundred. Be careful that you don't say, "between four *hundred* and five hundred." Have a friend time you and, when she says "Go," just count up to ten. After all, 10 is between 4 and 500!

LOWEST TERMS

Here's a much easier way to reduce fractions. You don't even have to divide. Ask your math teacher if you can reduce all your fractions this way!

Example

Reduce $\frac{8}{14}$

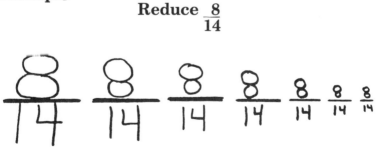

Warning: Don't try this on a test unless your math teacher has a *great* sense of humor!

HALF AND HALF

Hand your friend a dollar and tell her she can have it if she can fold it in half seven times by alternately folding the length in half and then the width. Don't worry about losing that dollar. No matter how hard she tries, she will not be able to make that seventh fold.

The Secret

The dollar will be half as big every time it is folded. So, after the sixth fold, it will be very small and hard to handle. Also, the number of layers doubles with every fold. After six folds, your friend will be trying to fold 64 layers of paper!

RIDICULOUS REDUCING

$$\frac{1\cancel{9}}{\cancel{9}5} = \frac{1}{5} \qquad \frac{1\cancel{6}}{\cancel{6}4} = \frac{1}{4} \qquad \frac{2\cancel{6}}{\cancel{6}5} = \frac{2}{5} \qquad \frac{4\cancel{9}}{\cancel{9}8} = \frac{4}{8} = \frac{1}{2}$$

Warning: These four fractions are special cases and this ridiculous method of reducing only works for them! If you reduce the fractions on your homework this way, you will get them all wrong!

62

5.
ARITHMETRICKS

These amazing number tricks are fun to watch and even more fun to perform for others. They are easy to learn and, if you follow the steps carefully, they practically work themselves.

Practice a trick until you have successfully worked it through two or three times. Then you are ready to perform it for your friends. Be sure to work the trick *slowly* so that you don't make careless errors.

Remember, magicians never reveal their secrets. When someone asks you how you did a trick, just say, "Very well!" Also, don't repeat a trick for the same person. They might figure out how you did the trick if they see it a second time. Show them another trick instead and they will be even more amazed!

63

COIN CAPER

Your friend removes some coins from a bowl when your back is turned. After performing some number magic, you are able to disclose the number of coins that are hidden in her hand!

Materials

20 coins   A small bowl

Presentation

Example

1. Put a bowl of 20 coins on the table, and then turn your back. Ask your friend to remove any number of coins from 1 to 9 and put them in her pocket.

**She removes
7 coins**

2. Tell her to count the number of coins that remain in the bowl.

**20 − 7 = 13
remain**

3. Ask her to find the sum of the digits of that number.

13 → 1 + 3 = 4

4. Tell her to remove that number of coins from the bowl and put those in her pocket too.

**She removes 4
more coins**

5. Ask her to remove any number of coins from the bowl and hide them in her *hand*.

She hides 6

6. When you turn around, take one of the coins out of the bowl. Hold it to your forehead and pretend to be in deep thought for a few seconds. Then reveal the number of coins that your friend is hiding in her hand!

How to Do It

When you turn around, secretly count the number of coins that remain in the bowl. Just subtract that number from 9. That difference is the number of coins that she is hiding in her hand!

9 − 3 coins in the bowl = 6 coins in her hand

An Exception

If your friend hides 9 coins in her hand and there are no coins left in the bowl, hold the bowl to your forehead.

The Secret

This trick uses a mathematical procedure called casting out nines. The first subtraction results in a number between 10 and 20. Any number between 10 and 20 minus the sum of its digits always equals 9.

A Variation

You can also tell her how many coins are in her pocket. It will always be 11!

RIDDLE ME

Why are 1980 U.S. pennies worth almost $20.00?

1,980 pennies = $19.80, which is almost $20.00!

ROYAL HEADACHE

Your friends will be amazed when you correctly predict which card will be chosen from the 20 cards on the table!

Materials

Paper and pencil   An envelope
A deck of playing cards

Preparation

Use 20 cards to make a figure 9 on the table. The values of the cards are not important but be sure that the suits are in the same order as shown in the diagram. Put the King of Hearts where the × is in the diagram.

Write "YOU WILL CHOOSE THE KING WHO HAS A SWORD STUCK IN HIS LEFT EAR!" on a piece of paper and seal it inside an envelope.

66

Presentation

1. Tell your friend that you have predicted which card he will choose and that you have sealed the prediction inside an envelope.

2. Ask him to think of any counting number *between* 5 and 20. (*Caution:* This number must be greater than 5.) Tell him to start counting from the end of the 9's tail. (The first card is counted as number 1.) He should continue counting up and around counterclockwise until he gets to his number. Tell him to keep his finger on that card.

3. Remove the 5 cards from the 9's tail and put them aside, leaving only a circle.

4. Now ask your friend to count in the opposite direction—clockwise—around the circle until he gets to his number. (The card that his finger is on is counted as number 1.)

5. Remove the 5 Club cards from the circle.

6. Tell him to count 6 cards in either direction. (Again, the card that his finger is on is number 1.) No matter which direction he goes, he will end up on the King of Hearts!

7. Finally, remind your friend that he was free to choose any number. Then open up your prediction and show him what you wrote. He won't believe his eyes. He will think that you have E.S.P.!

The Secret

When you count one way around a circle and then count that same number in the opposite direction, you always end up in the same place. The 9's tail helps hide this secret.

NUMBER SPIRITS

Your friend randomly chooses any 3-digit number, and then works a few problems on a calculator. When the Number Spirits' magic dust is rubbed on your lower arm, his final total mysteriously appears!

Materials

A calculator	Paper and pencil
Ground cinnamon	A glue stick

Preparation

Put a small amount of cinnamon or any dark spice in a small container. This is the Number Spirits' magic dust.

Write the number 1089 on the inside of your lower arm with a glue stick. The number should be invisible yet remain sticky.

Presentation   Example

1. Tell a friend to write any 3-digit number on a piece of paper without letting you see it. Tell him that the first digit must be *at least 2 greater* than the last digit.

831

2. Ask him to reverse the 3 digits and write this new number (138) below the first number. Have him subtract the two numbers on a calculator.

$$\begin{array}{r} 831 \\ -\ 138 \\ \hline 693 \end{array}$$

3. Tell him to reverse this difference and add this new number (396) to the calculator total.

$$\begin{array}{r} 693 \\ +\ 396 \\ \hline 1089 \end{array}$$

4. Remind your friend that he was free to choose any 3-digit number, and then ask him for his final total. Then summon the Number Spirits. Ask them to make your friend's final total magically appear as you sprinkle their magic dust on your lower arm. Perform some hocus-pocus as you rub the magic dust around. Blow off the excess dust and, like magic, the number 1089 mysteriously appears!

The Secret

It does not matter which 3-digit number your friend starts with. If he does the arithmetic correctly, the final total will always be 1089!

MATHEMATICAL ODDITY

Which sum is greater? Don't use a calculator.

987654321		123456789
87654321		12345678
7654321		1234567
654321		123456
54321	or	12345
4321		1234
321		123
21		12
+ 1		+1

IDENTICAL TWINS

Your friend randomly chooses any card on the table. He will be amazed when your prediction is opened and it matches his card!

Materials
Two decks of cards
An envelope

A coin

Preparation
Secretly seal an Ace of Hearts from a second deck in an envelope.

Place nine cards on the table in front of your friend. Be sure that they are in the *same order* as shown in the diagram.

Sit across the table from your friend, and put something between the two of you so that you cannot see the cards.

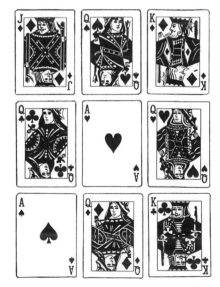

Presentation

Tell your friend that you have predicted which card he will choose and that you have sealed the prediction inside an envelope.

Ask him to place the coin on top of any of the four Queens. Tell him that he will be free to move that coin wherever he wants, but at the end of the trick, it will be sitting on your predicted card.

Explain that he can move the coin horizontally, vertically, forward or backwards, but *never diagonally*. Also, he cannot skip over cards. Make sure that the coin is on any Queen and then tell your friend to:

1. Move 6 times and then remove the Jack of Diamonds.

2. Move 3 times and then remove the Queen of Spades.

3. Move 2 times and then remove the Queen of Clubs.

4. Move 3 times and then remove the King of Diamonds and the Ace of Spades.

5. Move 2 times and then remove the King of Clubs.

6. Move 1 time and then remove the two red Queens.

If your friend followed your instructions, the coin will be on the Ace of Hearts!

Remind your friend that he was free to move the coin wherever he wanted. Then open your prediction and show him that the two cards are identical!

The Secret

There are only certain cards that you can land on when you move an even number or an odd number of times. Those cards that you *cannot* land on are removed. In the end, every card is removed except the Ace of Hearts.

SUPERMAN

You can prove to your friends that you have the power to see through solid objects by adding the *bottoms* of 5 dice!

Materials

5 dice

Presentation

1. Tell your friend that you are going to look through the dice and find the sum of the bottom numbers.

2. Throw 5 dice on the table.

3. Pretend that you can see through the dice all the way down to the bottom numbers. (What you are really doing is finding the sum of the top numbers.)

4. Announce the total of the 5 bottom numbers. (Just subtract the sum of the top numbers from 35.) Then

carefully turn over the 5 dice and add the bottom numbers. Your friend won't believe her eyes!

Example

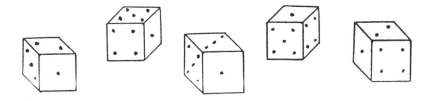

Sum of the top numbers = 13
35 − 13 = 22
So, the sum of the bottom numbers is 22!

The Secret

On any die, the sum of the top number and the bottom number is 7. So, if 5 dice are thrown, the total of all the top numbers and bottom numbers is:

$$5 \times 7 = 35$$
Dice   Total

A Variation

Use a different number of dice and subtract the sum of the top numbers from a different number than 35. To find that number, just multiply the number of dice by 7.

6.
CALCULATOR RIDDLES

The calculator that you own is a remarkable little machine. You've always known that it can perform mathematical calculations faster and with more accuracy than most humans, but did you know that it can also talk?

Yes, it's true! Your calculator will talk to you if you push the right buttons. For example, your calculator will tell you its name if you push clear and then *carefully* push $353 \times 9 \times 100 + 18 =$. Just turn your calculator *upside down*, and it will tell you!

Now that you and your calculator have been properly introduced, it's time to have some fun! Use the calculator alphabet below to help you find the answers to the math jokes and math riddles in this section. If you don't understand an answer, look at the explanation in the back of the book or just ask your calculator!

THE CALCULATOR ALPHABET

Upside-down numbers:	0 1 2 3 4 5 6 7 8 9
Letters:	O I Z E h S g L B G

1. What is the only thing that gets larger the more you take away?

$$25{,}000 - 68 - 952 - 8{,}956 - 11{,}320 =$$

2. Which has fewer legs, a goose or no goose?

$$25.009 \div .001 + 10{,}000 =$$

3. Picture these U.S. coins: a nickel, a penny, and a dime. OK? Ellie's parents have 3 children. One is Nick and another is Penny. Who is the third?

$$.05 \div .01 \div .10 \times 3 \times 211 + 123 =$$

4. How many legs does a barbershop quartet have?

$$2 \times 2 \times 2 \times 10 \times 70 + 338 - .09 =$$

5. A pet store owner has 17 eels. All but 9 were sold. How many eels does the owner have left?

$$337.8 \times 17 - 9 =$$

6. Who weighs more, Lee the 5-foot (152 cm) butcher or Bob the 7-foot (213 cm) wrestler?

$$5 \times 7 \times 10 - 13 =$$

7. A doctor gave you three pills and said to take one every half hour. How long will the pills last?

$$3 \times .5 + 2.6 =$$

8. Which would you rather have, an old one-hundred-dollar bill or a brand-new one?

$$100 \times 77 + 118.001 - 100 =$$

9. Bob and Bill took a dividing test in school. Bob wore glasses and Bill did not. Who got a higher score on the test?

$$10 \times 10 \times 10 - 200 + 8 =$$

10. How many seconds are in a year?

$$31{,}557{,}600 \div 1{,}000{,}000 - 26.3476 =$$

11. A barrel of water weighed 100 kilograms, but after somebody put something in it, it weighed only 25 kilograms. What was put in the barrel?

$$500 \times 100 + 4{,}000 - 300 + 4 =$$

12. Bill subtracted numbers for 20 minutes, Bess multiplied them, and Leslie added them.

Who was more exhausted when they finished?

$$9 + 57 + 868 + 7{,}920 + 93{,}208 + 215{,}475 =$$

Who went into debt when they were finished?

$$17{,}865 - 9{,}438 - 607 - 95 - 7 =$$

Who got the most work done in 20 minutes?

$$.3 \times 2 \times 2.6 \times 20 \times 7.1 \times 25 =$$

13. What number did the math teacher bring the student who fainted?

$$222 \times .2 \div 2 - .2 - 20 =$$

14. What is the largest number that will fit in your calculator's display?

$$99{,}999{,}999 \div 9 - 11{,}058{,}162 + 656{,}060 =$$

15. Bob says that only one month has 28 days. His boss says that there are more. Who is right?

$$28 \times 29 \times 30 + 31 - 18{,}882.486 =$$

16. What did seven do that made all the other numbers afraid of it?

$$7 \times .07 \div .7 \times 7 + 1.9 =$$

17. What number never tells the truth when it is resting?

$$223,314 \div 7 \div 2 \div 3 =$$

18. How much dirt is in a hole that is 5-feet deep, 2-feet wide, and 3-feet long?

I REALLY DIG THIS!

$$5 \times 2 \times 3 - 30 =$$

19. Take two eggs from three eggs and what do you have?

$$9,992 \times .2 \times 3 - 2 =$$

20. What part of a lame dog reminds you of what happens when you start adding 37 and 26?

$$224 \times 25 - 25.486 + 37 + 26 =$$

7.
WORDLES

Above is an example of a wordle. Wordles are fun puzzles that represent a familiar word or phrase. Notice that the word LONG is under the word WEAR, so this wordle is "Long Underwear!"

Here is another example:

HOROBOD

Notice that there are two words mixed together. The word ROB is in the word HOOD so this wordle is "Robin Hood!"

Now that you know how to solve wordles, you are ready to start. Each wordle in this section represents a common math word or math phrase. Have fun solving each puzzle, and then check in the back of the book to see if you are right. And, once you know the answers, add to your fun by sharing the wordles with your family and friends!

1.

```
77777  7777  7777  7   7
  7     7     7    77   7
  7     77    77    7  77
  7      7     7    7   77
  7    7777  7777   7    7
```

2.

g
n
i
d
n
u
o
r

3.

```
      G
  H       R
    P    A
```

4.

angle
angle
angle

5.

DIVISION

6.

```
    I T
M
  A   T
G N     I
```

7.

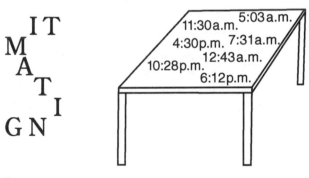

5:03a.m.
11:30a.m.
4:30p.m. 7:31a.m.
12:43a.m.
10:28p.m.
6:12p.m.

8.

NUMBERNUMBERNUMBERNUMBER

82

9.

10.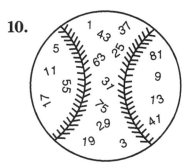

11. **0-144**

12. **TERMS**
TERMS
TERMS
TERMS
TERMS

13.

14. TpoEsiGtiEveR

15. **GNITNUOC**

16.

17.
P   T
O N N
N E
N E
P O N
P   T

18. **TER10%EST**

19. Q QUAL
U
  QUAL
A
L QUAL

20.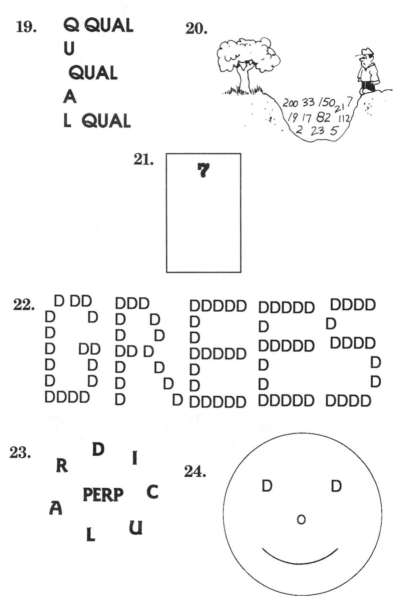

200 33 /50₂₁ 7
19 17 82 112
2 23 5

21.

7

22.

```
 D DD     DDD       DDDDD  DDDDD   DDDD
D     D   D    D    D      D       D
D         D      D  D      DDDDD  DDDD
D    DD   DD D      DDDDD   D      D
D     D   D    D    D      D              D
D     D   D      D  D      D              D
DDDD      D        D DDDDD  DDDDD  DDDD
```

23.

```
    D        I
 R
   PERP   C
A
   L    U
```

24.

```
    D      D

       o
```

25.   "DECIMAL" "DECIMAL" "DECIMAL"

26.

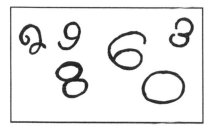

27.

one another
one another
one another
one another
one another
one another

28.

allel lines   allel lines

29.

4 4 4 4 4 4 4
4
4
4
4

30.

1,000,000

31.

ZZZZZZZZZZZZZZZZZZZZZZZZZZZZZZZ

32.

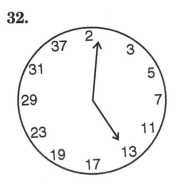

33.

34.

$$\frac{0}{10°}$$
$$87°$$
$$46°$$

35.

R O
T O

36.

HEIFAIRGHT

37.

PLY PLY PLY PLY PLY
PLY PLY PLY PLY PLY
PLY PLYPLY PLY PLY
PLY PLY PLY PLY PLY
PLY PLY PLY PLYPLY
PLY PLY PLY PLY PLY
PLY PLY PLY PLY PLY

38.

SECT SECT

8.
BRAINTEASERS

Brainteasers are challenging puzzles that require a little extra thinking. These fascinating mind bafflers are fun to solve and will help you develop important thinking skills that will last a lifetime.

The puzzles are organized from the easiest to the hardest, so choose those puzzles that are right for you. You might not be able to find the answer quickly, so be patient and keep trying. Don't just give up and look in the back of the book for the answer. If you need help with a puzzle, turn the page upside down, look at the hint, and then try again.

Problems don't always have just one answer, so yours might be different from the one in the back of the book. Also, it's okay if you use a different strategy to get a correct answer. You're a good problem solver when you think a problem through and find your own solution. And remember, once you know the answers, it's even more fun to share these brainteasers with your family and friends!

1. BOTTOMS UP

In exactly three moves, turn over glasses two at a time and end up with all the glasses upside down. Every glass must be turned over at least once.

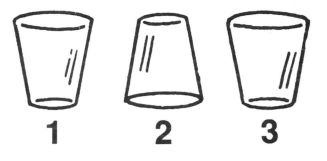

1   **2**   **3**

Turn over glass 1 and glass 2 on the first move.

2. CHECKMATE

Two friends were playing chess. They played five games. Each friend won five games and there were no ties. How can this be?

Think about the number of people who could be playing.

88

3. ON EDGE

When you drop a flat toothpick, it will land on one side or the other. How is it possible to have the toothpick land on one of its edges?

Something about the toothpick has to change.

4. KILLER

Killer is a ferocious guard dog who follows your every move and is tied to a tree with a long chain. Your basketball rolled away and ended up near the tree. How can you safely get your ball back without harming the dog?

Killer follows your every move. So how could you shorten the chain between him and the tree?

5. WHAT GOES UP MUST COME DOWN

You fall off a 20-foot (6 m) ladder and land on a hard concrete driveway, but you do not get hurt! Why not?

Think about *where* you could be standing on the ladder.

6. COIN SANDWICH

How can you remove the middle coin from between the other two coins without anything touching or hitting it?

Can you get a different coin in the middle?

7. MOOOOOVE IT

Can you make the top row look exactly like the bottom row by moving only one glass of chocolate milk?

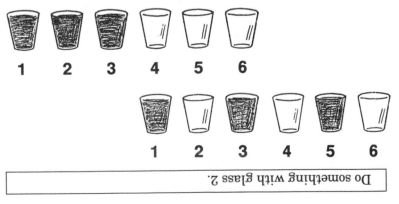

Do something with glass 2.

8. THIS IS NO YOLK

You are standing on a hard concrete floor and you have no cushioning to use. How can you drop a raw egg 4 feet (120 cm) without breaking it?

Air will not break the egg.

9. ROW, ROW, ROW YOUR BOAT

A girl was travelling back from town with a fox, a duck, and a sack of corn. She came to a river which she had to cross in a rowboat. But the boat was so small that it could only hold the girl and one other thing. She figured that she would have to make several trips. But she couldn't leave the fox alone with the duck because the fox would eat the duck. She couldn't leave the duck alone with the corn because the duck would eat the corn. How could the girl take everything across the river safely? Draw a diagram to help you find the solution.

She takes the duck across first.

10. THIS DOESN'T MAKE CENTS

Two U.S. coins total 30¢, but one is not a nickel. What are the two coins?

Think about the wording: *one* is not a nickel.

11. GO FISH

What is the *smallest* number of fish that can swim in this formation: 2 fish in front of a fish, 2 fish behind a fish, and a fish between 2 fish?

Draw a sketch.

12. ODD, ISN'T IT?

How can you put ten coins in three glasses so that each glass has an odd number of coins?

A glass can be put inside another glass.

13. BOOMERANG

You throw a ball as hard as you can. It doesn't hit anything and nothing is attached to it. Yet, the ball comes right back to you! How can this be?

Which direction can you throw a ball and have it come back to you?

14. GET THE POINT?

Using only paper and pencil, draw a circle with a point in the middle. The point cannot be connected to the circle, and you cannot lift your pencil off of the paper.

Try folding the paper and using both sides.

15. ELLIE VATOR

Ellie lives on the nineteenth floor of an apartment building. Whenever she gets into the elevator on the first floor, she presses the button for the fourth floor, where she gets out and walks the rest of the way up. When she leaves her apartment, however, she takes the elevator all the way down. She would rather ride than walk so then why does she do this?

Think about *how* the buttons are placed on the wall inside the elevator.

16. PERFECT SQUARE

Move only one wooden match to form a square.

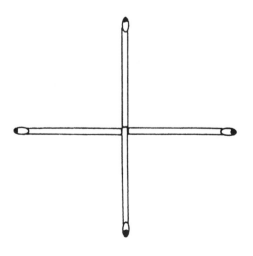

It is a very small square.

94

17. DO KNOT LET GO

Hold one end of a piece of rope or string in each hand and tie a knot in the middle without letting go of the two ends.

Start with your arms tied in a knot.

18. TIGHT FIT

Cut a hole in the center of an index card just big enough for a small coin to pass through. How can you push a larger coin through the hole without tearing the index card?

You can also use a pencil.

95

19. FASTER THAN THE SPEED OF LIGHT

Your light switch is way across the room from your bed. Yet you are able to turn off your light switch, and then jump into bed before your room gets dark. There are no timers used. How is this possible?

Think about *when* you could jump into bed before your room gets dark.

20. THAT'S USING YOUR HEAD

Change the top row and the bottom row to all tails and the middle row to all heads. You are allowed to touch only one coin.

Start by picking up the middle coin in the bottom row.

9.
CALCULATOR CONJURING

Did you know that your calculator is a talented magician? If you enter the correct numbers, it will perform many magic tricks for you!

All of the magic tricks in this chapter are performed on an ordinary calculator. The tricks are organized from the easiest to the hardest, so choose those that are right for you. They are easy to learn and perform but you still need to practice them by yourself first. You should work a trick through successfully two or three times before you perform it for others.

You have to be very careful, however, and make sure you push the right buttons or the trick will not work. Perform each trick *slowly* so that you don't make careless errors.

Finally, remember that magicians never reveal their secrets. If someone asks you how you did a trick, just say, "Very carefully!" If they still question you, tell them to ask your calculator!

SEVEN-UP

You have the luckiest calculator in the world. No matter which number your friend enters, it is magically transformed into the lucky number 7!

Materials
A calculator

Presentation
Hand your friend the calculator and have her:

	Example
1. Enter any number that is easy to remember. (This number must be less than 8 digits.)	**123**
2. Double that number.	$123 \times 2 = 246$
3. Subtract 16 from that answer.	$246 - 16 = 230$
4. Multiply that result by 4.	$230 \times 4 = 920$
5. Divide that total by 8.	$920 \div 8 = 115$
6. Add 15 to that answer.	$115 + 15 = 130$
7. Subtract her original number from that result.	$130 - 123 = 7$

This trick can be repeated several times with the same friend. No matter which number she starts with, the final answer will always end up "lucky"!

The Secret

All of the tricks in this chapter were written using a branch of mathematics called algebra. In this trick, if all of the operations are carefully performed, your friend's original number is eliminated. Adding 15 in Step 6 guarantees that the final total will always be 7.

A Variation

Experiment by adding a different number in Step 6 and the final total will be a different number.

PAIR-A-DICE

Your friend rolls 2 dice when you are not looking. After he works a few problems on a calculator, you are able to reveal the two top numbers on the dice!

Materials

2 dice   A calculator
Paper and pencil

Presentation

Example

When your back is turned,
have a friend:

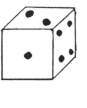

1. Roll two dice.

2. Multiply the top number on
the first die by 5, using a
calculator or paper and pencil.

$$\underline{2} \times 5 = 10$$

3. Add 12 to that answer.

$$10 + 12 = 22$$

4. Double that total.

$$22 \times 2 = 44$$

5. Add that result to the top
number on the second die.

$$44 + \underline{6} = 50$$

6. Add 15 to that answer.

$$50 + 15 = 65$$

Finally, ask your friend for his final total. Just subtract
39 and the top numbers on the dice will magically
appear!

$$
\begin{array}{r}
6\,5 \\
-\,3\,9 \\
\hline
\underline{2}\,\underline{6} \\
\end{array}
$$

1st 2nd
die die

The Secret

Multiplying by 5 and then doubling is just like multiplying by 10. This puts the number on the first die in the
tens place. Adding the number on the second die puts
that number in the ones place. Every other operation is
mathematical hocus-pocus and adds an extra 39 to the
total. Subtracting this 39 reveals the two top numbers
on the dice.

SPECIAL FRIEND

Your friend will think that you possess supernatural powers when you correctly reveal the name that she has chosen from a list of her friends!

Materials

A calculator   Paper and pencil

Presentation

Ask your friend to make a list of at least five of her friends' names. Tell her to number each name.

Then ask her to:

	Example
1. Write the number of a "special" friend on a piece of paper without showing you.	**Friend #8**
2. Multiply that number by 5.	$8 \times 5 = 40$
3. Add 5 to that result.	$40 + 5 = 45$
4. Double that answer.	$45 \times 2 = 90$
5. Add 45 to that total.	$90 + 45 = 135$

6. Cross off the last digit of that
answer.

13̶5̶

7. Add 44 to that result.

$$13 + 44 = 57$$

Finally, ask your friend for her final total. Just subtract 49 and the number of her special friend will magically appear!

$$
\begin{array}{r}
57 \\
-49 \\
\hline
\end{array}
$$

Friend #8 → **8**

The Secret

If all of the operations are carefully performed, the final total will always be 49 more than the special friend's number. Subtracting 49 reveals that number.

BIRTHDAY SURPRISE

You will be able to divulge anyone's age and the year they were born by simply performing some number magic on a calculator!

Materials

A calculator

Presentation

Hand someone a calculator and ask her to:

Example
Year Born: 1955
Age: 39

1. Enter the year that she was born, without letting you see it.

1955

2. Multiply that year by 2.

$$1955 \times 2 = 3{,}910$$

3. Add the number of months in a year.

$$3{,}910 + 12 = 3{,}922$$

4. Multiply that total by 50.

$$3{,}922 \times 50 = 196{,}100$$

5. Add her age to that result.

$$196{,}100 + 39 = 196{,}139$$

6. Add the number of days in a year.

$$196{,}139 + 365 = 196{,}504$$

Finally, tell her to hand you the calculator with the final total. Just subtract 965, and the year that she was born and her age will magically appear!

$$
\begin{array}{r}
1\,965\,04 \\
-\quad\ 9\,65 \\
\hline
1\,955\,39
\end{array}
$$

Year Age
Born

Exceptions

If the person's age is less than 10, the tens place will be 0.

Example: 198905 = $\underline{1\,9\,8\,9}\ \underline{0\,5}$, so age = 5

If it happens to be a leap year, add 366 in Step 6 and then subtract 966 from the final total.

The Secret

Multiplying the year by 2 and then by 50 is just like multiplying by 100. This moves the year over to and to the left of the hundreds place. Adding the age puts that number in the last two places. Every other operation is mathematical hocus-pocus and adds an extra 965 to the total. Subtracting this 965 reveals the year born and age.

LAST LAUGH

A card from a second deck is sealed in an envelope. You predict that this card will match your friend's chosen card. At the end it appears as though you have made a mistake, but you always end up getting the last laugh!

Materials

A calculator   2 decks of playing cards
An envelope

Preparation

Tear off the top half of the 10 of Diamonds from an old deck of cards so that only five of the ten diamonds are showing. Seal this card in an envelope.

Put the 5 of Diamonds in the eleventh position down from the top of the deck.

Presentation

Tell your friend that he will randomly select a card from the deck and that the card in the envelope will match his selected card.

Hand your friend the calculator and have him:

1. Enter his address or any other counting number that is easy to remember. (This number must be less than 7 digits.)   **Example**   **41**

2. Multiply that number by 100.   **41 × 100 = 4100**

3. Subtract his original number from that answer.   **4100 − 41 = 4059**

4. Divide that total by his original number. $4059 \div 41 = 99$

5. Divide that result by 9. $99 \div 9 = 11$

Finally, remind your friend that he was free to choose any number. Then ask him for his final total. Have him count down that many cards in the deck and turn over the eleventh card, the 5 of Diamonds.

Open up the envelope and slowly slide out the 10 of Diamonds, being careful not to show the missing bottom. Your friend will think that you have made a mistake. Then slide the card all the way out and have him count the diamonds. Your prediction is correct after all because there are only 5 diamonds!

The Secret

Multiplying any counting number by 100, subtracting the number, and then dividing by the number always equals 99. Finally, dividing by 9 results in 11 for the final total.

DOUBLE TROUBLE

Pick any 1-, 2-, or 3-digit number. See what happens when you multiply that number by 7, then by 11, and finally by 13. After you get the answer, clear your calculator. Then multiply $7 \times 11 \times 13$ and you will see why it works.

106

ORANGE ELEPHANT

Your friends are amazed with your mystical powers when you look into the future and reveal their deepest thoughts.

Materials

A calculator   Paper and pencil
An envelope

Preparation

Write "AN ORANGE ELEPHANT FROM FLORIDA" on a piece of paper and seal it inside an envelope.

Presentation

Tell your friend that you have predicted the outcome of this trick and that you have sealed the prediction inside an envelope.

    Then hand her the calculator and ask her to:

1. Enter any number that is easy to remember in the calculator without letting you see it. (This number must be less than 8 digits.)

Example

99

2. Multiply that number by 4. $99 \times 4 = 396$

3. Add 25 to that result. $396 + 25 = 421$

4. Double that answer. $421 \times 2 = 842$

5. Subtract 2 from that total. $842 - 2 = 840$

6. Divide that result by 8. $840 \div 8 = 105$

7. Subtract her original number
from that total. $105 - 99 = 6$

Ask your friend to write her
final result on a piece of paper.   **6**

Tell her to number the letters of
the alphabet (A = 1, B = 2, C = 3,
etc.) and write down the letter
that equals her number.   **6 = F**

Ask her to write down the name
of a U.S. state that starts with
that letter.   **F = Florida**

Tell her to look at the third letter
of that state and write down a ba-
sic color that starts with that
letter.   **o = orange**

Ask her to look at the last letter
of that color and write down the
name of a very large animal that
starts with that letter.   **e = elephant**

Finally, open up your prediction. Unbelievably, it should
match her 3 answers.

An **orange elephant** from **Florida!**

The Secret

If all of the operations are carefully performed, your friend's original number is eliminated and the final total will always be 6.

A Variation

Instead of making a prediction, have your friend concentrate on her three answers and then pretend that you are reading her mind.

CONCEALED COIN

This is a trick you can do for a group of your friends or relatives. When your back is turned, someone hides a coin in one of their hands. After you work some number magic, you are able to disclose who has the coin and which hand it is hiding in!

Materials

A calculator   A coin
Paper and pencil

Presentation

Pick one of your friends to be your assistant, and then number the rest of your friends starting with number 1. While your back is turned, have your assistant hide a coin in someone's hand. Tell him to write down that person's number and the hand that is hiding the coin. Tell everyone else to make fists with their hands.

Hand your assistant the calculator and have him:

Example
Friend #4
Right Hand

1. Enter the number of the person who has the coin. **4**

2. Multiply that number by 5. $4 \times 5 = 20$

3. Add 13 to that answer. $20 + 13 = 33$

4. Multiply that result by 4. $33 \times 4 = 132$

5. Add 88 to that total. $132 + 88 = 220$

6. Divide that answer by 2. $220 \div 2 = 110$

7. Add 4 if the coin is hidden in the left hand. Add 5 if the coin is hidden in the right hand. $110 + 5 = 115$

8. Add 50 to that result. $115 + 50 = 165$

Finally, ask your assistant to hand you the calculator

with the final total. Just subtract 123 and you will be able to find that coin!

$$165$$
$$-123$$

Person #4 → $\underline{4}\underline{2}$ ← Hand
1 = left
2 = right

An Exception

When you subtract 123 and get three digits, the first two digits are the number of the person.

Example: $$274$$
$$-123$$

Person #15 → $\underline{15}\,\underline{1}$ ← Left Hand

The Secret

Multiplying the person's number by 5 and 4 and then dividing by 2 is just like multiplying by 10. This moves the person's number over to and to the left of the tens place. Adding the hand puts that number in the ones place. Every other addition is mathematical hocus-pocus and adds an extra 123 to the total. Subtracting this 123 reveals the person's number and the correct hand.

RIDDLE ME

Why did the math book go on a diet?

It had a lot of fractions to reduce!

111

ANSWERS

3. PUZZLES

LINE BOGGLERS

Two-way Street   **Sum Time** $6+5=9???$

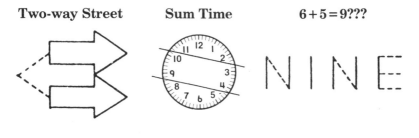

In Need of Repair   **Tunnels**   **Pepperoni Pizza**

$1 + 3 + 5 = 148$
OR
$1 + 3 + 5 \neq 148$

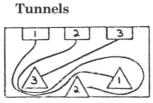

PENCIL PUZZLERS

1.

2.

3.

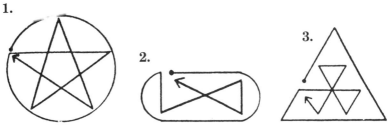

4.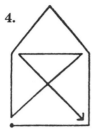

5.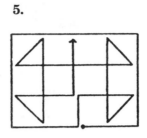

6.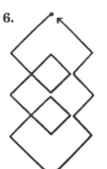

7.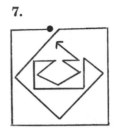

8.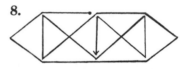

TOOTHPICK TEASERS

Aquarium

Architect   **Crisscross**

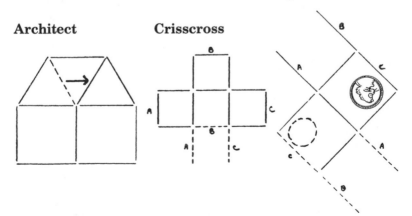

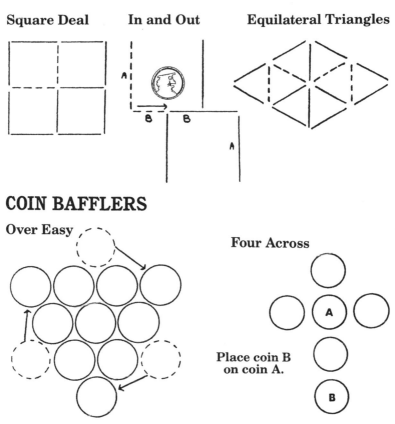

Square Deal **In and Out** **Equilateral Triangles**

COIN BAFFLERS

Over Easy

Four Across

Place coin B
on coin A.

Do Not Touch

You can remove the coin from the glass by just turning the page a third of a turn to the right.

Constellation

2 to 7
8 to 5 to 2
6 to 3 to 8 to 5
4 to 1 to 6 to 3 to 8
7 to 4 to 1 to 6
2 to 7 to 4
5 to 2

Coin Checkers

1. Slide H (heads) into empty space.
2. Jump H with a T (tails).
3. Slide T into new empty space.
4. Jump T with an H.
5. Jump other T with other H.
6. Slide T into empty space.
7. Jump H with a T.
8. Slide H just jumped into empty space.

115

NUMBER JUGGLING

Box Score

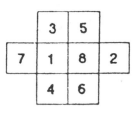

Wheel Numbers

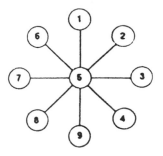

Bermuda Triangle

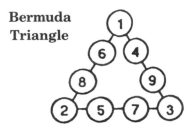

Troublesum

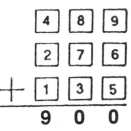

Magic Square

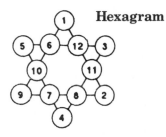

Hexagram

BRAIN BUSTERS

Stargazer

Box Score II

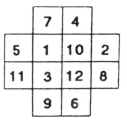

Windowpanes

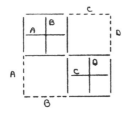

Dot to Dot

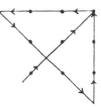

Tunnels II

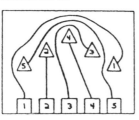

Tetrahedron

---

6. CALCULATOR RIDDLES

1. A hole. When you take away more dirt, the hole gets larger!

2. A goose. A goose has 2 legs but no goose has 4 legs!

3. Ellie. They are her parents, so she must be one of their children!

4. 16 legs (the decimal point separates numbers and words). One of the four singers is a *ten*or and $10 + 2 + 2 + 2 = 16$!

5. 9 eels, because 9 eels were *not* sold!

6. Lee, the butcher. He weighs meat all day long!

7. 1 h (hour). The third pill will be taken one hour after the first pill!

8. ($)100 bill. It is worth $99 more than the new one ($1)!

9. Bob scored higher on the math test because glasses improve di *vision*!

10. 12s (seconds). January second, February second, March second, etc.!

11. Holes, so 75 kilograms of water leaked out!

12. Leslie. She was more exhausted because of all the numbers that she had to carry!
    Bill, because of all of the borrowing that he had to do!
    Bess, because she was so *product*ive!

13. 2. The math teacher brought the student to!

14. A googol. It has 101 digits!

15. His boss is right. *All* of the months have at least 28 days!

16. 8.9 (seven ate nine)!

17. The number 5,317. It *lies* when it is resting on its back!

18. 0. No matter how you turn the calculator, there is no dirt in a hole!

19. 2 eggs. You *took* 2 eggs so you *have* 2 eggs!

20. His legs, because he puts down 3 and carries 1!

7. WORDLES

1. seventeen (7 TEEN)
2. rounding up
3. circle graph
4. triangle (3 ANGLES)
5. long division
6. estimating (S TIMATING)
7. times table
8. number line
9. percent (PER cent)
10. odd ball
11. Oh gross! (144 = a gross)
12. reduced to lowest terms
13. sequence (C QUENCE)
14. positive integer (POSITIVE in TEGER)
15. counting backwards
16. rectangle (wrecked angle)
17. exponent (X PONENT)
18. 10% interest (10% in TEREST)

19. equal (E QUAL)
20. whole numbers (hole numbers)
21. Seven Up
22. degrees (D GREES)
23. perpendicular (PERP in DICULAR)
24. division (D vision)
25. repeating decimal
26. rounded numbers
27. six of one, half a dozen of another
28. parallel lines (pair ALLEL LINES)
29. forty (4 T)
30. one in a million
31. zero (Z row)
32. prime time
33. mixed numbers
34. three degrees below zero
35. square root
36. Fahrenheit (FAIR in HEIGHT)
37. multiply (multi PLY)
38. bisect (bi SECT)

8. BRAINTEASERS

1. Bottoms Up
1. Turn over glass 1 and glass 2.
2. Turn over glass 1 and glass 3.
3. Turn over glass 1 and glass 2.
See if you can find another solution.

2. Checkmate
The two friends were not playing each other. Each one was playing another friend.

3. On Edge
Before you drop the toothpick, make a right angle by folding it in the middle.

4. Killer
Run in a circular pattern just out of reach of the dog. Since he follows your every move, he will wind his chain tighter and tighter around the tree. When he runs out of chain, walk over and safely pick up your basketball.

5. What Goes Up Must Come Down
You were standing on the bottom rung of the ladder, or maybe the ladder was lying flat on the ground.

6. Coin Sandwich
Move one of the end coins to the opposite end of the row and a different coin will be in the middle.

7. Mooooove It
Pour the contents of glass 2 into glass 5 and then replace glass 2.

8. This Is No Yolk
Hold the egg up and drop it from a height of 5 feet (150 cm). The egg can then drop 4 feet (120 cm) through the air without breaking. It won't break until it hits the ground.

9. Row, Row, Row Your Boat
Here's one solution:
1. She takes the duck across.
2. She returns by herself and then takes the fox across.
3. She returns with the duck and then takes the corn across.
4. She returns by herself and then takes the duck across.

See if you can find a second solution.

10. This Doesn't Make Cents
The two coins are a quarter and a nickel. The quarter is not a nickel.

11. Go Fish
Three fish in a row.

12. Odd, Isn't It?
Here's one solution:
Put 1 coin in the first glass, 4 in the second glass, and 5 in the third glass. Then pick up the first glass and set it *inside* the second. Now the second glass has a total of 5 coins.

13. Boomerang
Throw the ball straight up in the air and gravity will return it to you.

14. Get the Point?

 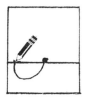 

Fold up the bottom fourth of the paper, and then draw a point in the center.

Without lifting your pencil off of the paper, draw a loop on the *folded part* over to one side.

Open up the paper and then complete the circle.

15. Ellie Vator

Ellie is a small child and can only reach as high as the fourth-floor button. She can go all the way down because she has no trouble reaching the first-floor button.

16. Perfect Square

Gently move the bottom match down a little and a tiny square will form between the ends of the matches.

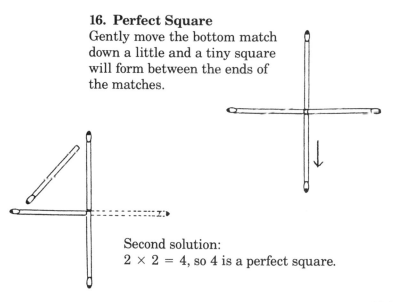

Second solution:
$2 \times 2 = 4$, so 4 is a perfect square.

121

17. Do Knot Let Go
Lay the rope on the table, *fold your arms*, and then pick up the ends of the rope. Do not let go of the ends of the rope as you unfold your arms, and the knot will be transferred from your folded arms to the rope.

18. Tight Fit
Lay the larger coin on the table. Then take a pencil, put it *through the hole* in the index card, and *push the larger coin* with the pencil.

19. Faster than the Speed of Light
Go to bed when it is still light outside and you will be in bed before the room gets dark.

20. That's Using Your Head
Remove the bottom middle coin and flip it over to tails. Then use it to push each of the other two middle coins down one row. Finally, put that coin in the middle of the top row.

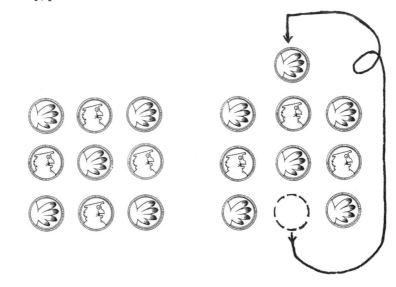

GLOSSARY

algebra A mathematical language that uses letters along with numbers. $2x - 5 = 15$ is an example of an algebra problem.

arithmetricks A collection of number-magic tricks.

array An orderly arrangement of objects in rows and columns.

between Example: A number is between 10 and 20 when it is greater than 10 and less than 20.

bisect To divide into two congruent parts.

boxcars Two 6's when two dice are rolled.

casting out nines A process that removes groups of nine from a number. Example: $25 - 9 = 16$ and $16 - 9 = 7$. Quick way: $25 \rightarrow 2 + 5 = 7$

clockwise The direction that the hands on a clock move.

column Objects that are arranged vertically.

congruent Having the same size and shape.

consecutive numbers Numbers that are in order. Example: 5, 6, 7, and 8.

counterclockwise The opposite direction of clockwise.

counting number The numbers 1, 2, 3, 4, 5, ...

diagonal line A slanting line.

die (plural: dice) One of a set of dice.

difference The answer to a subtraction problem.

digit Any of the symbols 0 to 9. Example: 827 is a 3-digit number.

double Multiply by 2.

equation A mathematical sentence with an equals sign. Examples: $3 + 5 = 8$ or $x - 7 = 1$

equilateral triangle A triangle with three congruent sides.

even numbers The numbers 0, 2, 4, 6, 8, 10, ...

face cards The jacks, queens, and kings of playing cards.

factor A number that divides into another number exactly. Example: The factors of 12 are 1, 2, 3, 4, 6, and 12.

googol   The number 1 followed by 100 zeros.

hexagram   A star with six points, formed by two equilateral triangles placed one across the other.

hocus-pocus   Extra steps that are added to a magic trick that help hide the trick's secret. Also, extra showmanship that makes a trick more interesting.

horizontal line   A line that runs straight across from left to right.

hundreds place   Example: 479. The 4 is in the hundreds place.

integers   The numbers . . . , $-3, -2, -1, 0, 1, 2, 3, \ldots$.

key numbers   The numbers that lead to a win in a game of strategy.

magic square   An array of numbers where the sum of each row, column, and diagonal is the same.

million   A word name for 1,000,000.

mnemonic aid   Something that helps the memory.

Number Spirits   Mathematical ghosts.

odd numbers   The numbers 1, 3, 5, 7, 9, 11, ...

odds   The chances that one thing will happen rather than another.

ones place   Example: 479. The 9 is in the ones place.

perfect square   The product when a whole number is multiplied by itself. Example: $3 \times 3 = 9$, so 9 is a perfect square.

prime number   A whole number greater than 1 that has exactly two factors, 1 and itself. Examples: 2, 3, 5, 7, 11, 13, 17, . . .

probability   The chance that a certain thing will happen.

product   The answer to a multiplication problem.

quotient   The answer to a division problem.

random number   A number chosen by chance.

right angle   An angle that measures 90°. Example: The capital letter L has a right angle.

124

row   Objects that are arranged horizontally.

snake eyes   Two 1's when two dice are rolled.
sum   The answer to an addition problem.

tens place   Example: 479. The 7 is in the tens place.
tetrahedron   The most common tetrahedron is a pyramid, whose base and three sides are all equilateral triangles.

vertex (plural: vertices)   The point where lines meet to form an angle.
vertical line   A line that runs straight up and down.

whole numbers   The numbers 0, 1, 2, 3, 4, 5, ...

year   Twelve months or 365 days (366 days in a leap year).

INDEX

Page key: Puzzle or Game, *Answer.*

ABOUT THE AUTHOR

Raymond Blum has been a middle-level math teacher for over 20 years. In 1991, he authored the book *Mathemagic*, which is filled with dozens of number-magic tricks for children ages nine and up. He has been a speaker at numerous state and national math conferences where he shares his number tricks with other classroom teachers. For five years, he entertained professionally with his daughter, Katie. Their stage show was called "Raynbow and The Amazing Kaytee's Juggling & Magic Show." Now Ray performs a number-magic show for elementary and middle school children as "Professor Numbers." The Professor shows children the magical fun side of mathematics with his mathemagic and arithmetricks. Ray has won several awards and, in 1994, he was selected as Wisconsin's Teacher of the Year. Ray is currently teaching seventh-grade math at Whitehorse Middle School in Madison, Wisconsin.

ABOUT THE ARTIST

Jeff Sinclair is a cartoonist and humorous illustrator living in Vancouver, British Columbia, Canada. He has won several awards for cartoon design and is now self-publishing his own line of humorous, limited-edition prints and posters. Jeff and his wife, Karen, have two children, Brennan and Conner, and a large Great Dane, Coz.